CHRISTIAN McCAFFREY

NFL STAR

By Douglas Lynne

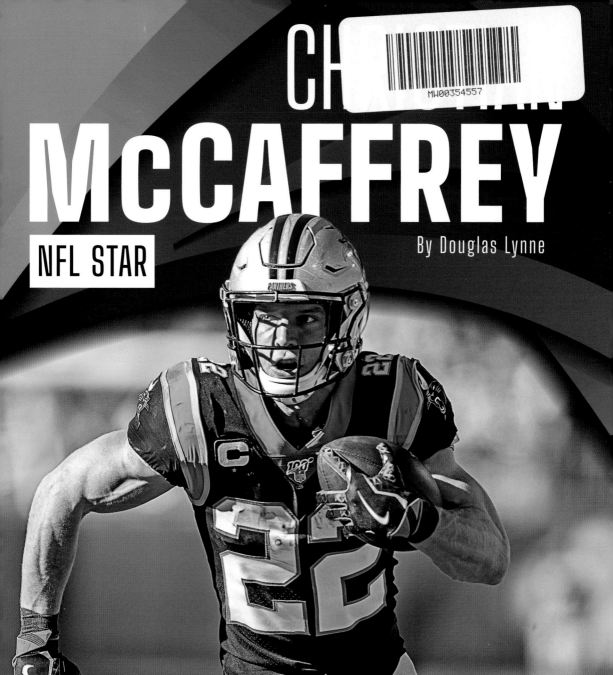

Book design by Jake Nordby
Cover design by Jake Nordby

Photographs ©: Tom DiPace/AP Images, cover, 1; Damian Strohmeyer/AP Images, 4; Mike McCarn/AP Images, 6–7, 21; Logan Bowles/AP Images, 9; David Zalubowski/AP Images, 10; Damon Tarver/Cal Sport Media/AP Images, 13; Chuck Burton/AP Images, 14; Steven King/Icon Sportswire, 17; Action Sports Photography/Shutterstock Images, 18, 23; Red Line Editorial, 22

Press Box Books, an imprint of Press Room Editions.

Library of Congress Control Number: 2020901617

ISBN
978-1-63494-222-5 (library bound)
978-1-63494-240-9 (paperback)
978-1-63494-258-4 (epub)
978-1-63494-276-8 (hosted ebook)

Distributed by North Star Editions, Inc.
2297 Waters Drive
Mendota Heights, MN 55120
www.northstareditions.com

Printed in the United States of America
082020

ABOUT THE AUTHOR

Douglas Lynne is a freelance writer. He spent many years working in the media, first in newspapers and later for online organizations, covering everything from breaking news to politics to entertainment to sports. He lives in Minneapolis, Minnesota.

TABLE OF CONTENTS

MR. DO IT ALL

1

Christian McCaffrey stood back and waited. His Carolina Panthers were deep in their own territory. The Jacksonville Jaguars defenders dug in their heels. They were ready to make a stop in the October 2019 game.

The Panthers snapped the ball. McCaffrey took the handoff five yards behind the line of scrimmage. Jaguars defenders closed in. McCaffrey had

Christian McCaffrey looks for room to run in a 2019 game.

 None of the Jaguars could catch McCaffrey.

to react quickly. He cut inside. A small gap was open between his blockers. McCaffrey squeezed through untouched. It was the perfect move. With no Jaguars in his way, the

star running back was loose. He sprinted 84 yards for the touchdown. It was his third of the day.

McCaffrey can do it all. He's fast. He's shifty. He's smart. He also has hands like a wide receiver.

RESCUE MISSION

In March 2018, McCaffrey was hiking near his hometown in Colorado. Suddenly, a nearby hiker slipped. "We basically saw a man fall off a cliff," McCaffrey recalled. The football player jumped into action, calling 9-1-1. One of McCaffrey's brothers helped bring the injured man to a safer spot. Their efforts helped save the man's life.

One thing McCaffrey doesn't do is get tired. He was all over the field that day. He ran the ball 19 times. The Panthers threw the ball his way eight times. He caught six of the passes. In the end, he finished with 176 rushing yards and 61 receiving yards. The combined 237 yards from scrimmage tied his own team record.

PANTHERS LEADERS
MOST YARDS FROM SCRIMMAGE IN A GAME

- **Christian McCaffrey, 237,** October 6, 2019
- **Christian McCaffrey, 237,** November 25, 2018
- **Jonathan Stewart, 222,** December 27, 2009
- **DeAngelo Williams, 213,** December 30, 2012
- **Christian McCaffrey, 209,** September 8, 2019

McCaffrey and his teammates had plenty to celebrate after they beat the Jaguars.

2

COLORADO KID

Christian Jackson McCaffrey was born on June 7, 1996, in Castle Rock, Colorado. That city is just south of Denver. Christian's dad, Ed McCaffrey, was a star wide receiver for the Denver Broncos. He played 13 seasons in the National Football League (NFL).

Christian grew up around the game. He showed promise from an early age. In high school he was an outstanding defensive

Christian, age 5, hangs out with his parents, Ed and Lisa.

back, wide receiver, and punter. But he was best known as a running back. Many college coaches wanted Christian to play for them. He picked Stanford University in California.

By his sophomore year in 2015, Christian was a star. He piled up 3,864 all-purpose yards. That stat includes rushing, receiving, and returning kicks. His efforts smashed the college record held by Hall of Fame running back Barry Sanders. Stanford's coach said Christian was like a Swiss Army knife. That means he was useful in many ways. He also was someone who could not just do a lot, but "do it extremely well."

Christian shows his receiving skills for Stanford in 2015.

Christian played one more year at Stanford. He gained nearly 2,000 total yards rushing and receiving. It was time for his next challenge. He decided to enter the NFL Draft.

GOING PRO

McCaffrey's college statistics were remarkable. Some NFL coaches were not convinced, though. Other backs were bigger or stronger or faster. Was McCaffrey good enough in any one area to truly thrive? The Carolina Panthers believed so. They selected him eighth overall in the 2017 draft.

The Panthers had built their offense around star quarterback Cam Newton.

McCaffrey meets the press after being drafted by the Panthers in 2017.

They believed McCaffrey would be the perfect sidekick. That proved to be right. And it showed right away in training camp. Teammates struggled to stop him. They couldn't wait to unleash McCaffrey on opponents.

It took some time for McCaffrey to get used to the NFL. But the rookie showed signs of what was to come. In his third game, he reached 100 receiving yards. In Week 14 he had 136 total yards. He gained 63 on the ground. He added 73 more in the air. That included a receiving touchdown. Most importantly, the Panthers ended the season in the playoffs.

McCaffrey had shown all the tools to be an offensive threat. He had lightning-quick feet. This made him hard to catch. But he also had soft hands. He could bring in passes like a wide receiver. All of this made him a matchup

As a rookie, McCaffrey had to adjust to the size and speed of NFL defenders.

McCaffrey came into his own during his second professional season.

nightmare for defenses. Put a linebacker on McCaffrey and he'd run right past him. Put a defensive back on McCaffrey and he'd run right through him. Even if defenders did everything right, McCaffrey could find ways to beat them.

As he did in college, McCaffrey broke out in his second year. He ended the season with 1,098 rushing yards. Only five players had more that year. None of those players also had more than 100 catches, though. In fact, no running back had ever caught more than 102 passes in a season. McCaffrey ended with 107.

In just two seasons, McCaffrey had shown off

EATING RIGHT

McCaffrey no doubt has amazing athletic talent. A strict diet helps, too. He worked with a chef to figure out which foods were helping—and hurting. The result was a custom meal plan. McCaffrey keeps his eating very simple. He also drinks 1.5 gallons (5.7 L) of water each day. "The less I think about meals and everything else, the more I can focus on my sport," he said.

his unique abilities. And he only got better. Throughout 2019 he continued to rack up yards. With two games left, he'd already set a career high in rushing yards. With 15 catches that game, he broke his own receiving record. Then, in the finale, he hit another milestone. McCaffrey crossed 1,000 receiving yards on the season. That made him just the third player with 1,000 yards both on the ground and in the air in the same season.

Some people doubted McCaffrey coming out of college. They had never seen anyone quite like him. Neither had the Panthers. And that proved to be a very good thing.

CHRISTIAN MCCAFFREY
2019 STATISTICS
- **Rushing:** 287 carries, 1,387 yards, 15 TDs
- **Receiving:** 116 catches, 1,005 yards, 4 TDs

All signs were positive through McCaffrey's first three NFL seasons.

TIMELINE MAP

1. **Castle Rock, Colorado: 1996**
   Christian Jackson McCaffrey is born on June 7.

2. **Highlands Ranch, Colorado: 2013**
   McCaffrey is named the top high school football player in Colorado.

3. **Stanford, California: 2015**
   As a sophomore, McCaffrey gains a college record 3,864 yards from scrimmage.

4. **Philadelphia, Pennsylvania: 2017**
   The Panthers select McCaffrey eighth in the NFL Draft.

5. **Charlotte, North Carolina: 2017**
   McCaffrey posts a Panthers rookie season record 1,086 yards from scrimmage.

6. **Charlotte, North Carolina: 2018**
   McCaffrey sets a team record with 237 yards from scrimmage against Seattle on November 25.

7. **Indianapolis, Indiana: 2019**
   McCaffrey catches 15 passes against the Colts on December 22.

8. **New Orleans, Louisiana: 2019**
   McCaffrey becomes the third NFL player to ever top 1,000 rushing yards and 1,000 receiving yards in the same season.

N

AT-A-GLANCE

CHRISTIAN MCCAFFREY

Birth date: June 7, 1996

Birthplace: Castle Rock, Colorado

Position: Running back

Height: 5 feet 11 inches

Weight: 205 pounds

Current team: Carolina Panthers (2017–)

Past team: Stanford Cardinal (2014–16)

Major awards: Pro Bowl (2019), First Team All-Pro (2019), Associated Press Player of the Year (2015), Pac-12 Offensive Player of the Year (2015), Colorado High School Player of the Year (2012, 2013)

Accurate through the 2019 season.

MORE INFORMATION

To learn more about Christian McCaffrey, go to **pressboxbooks.com/AllAccess**.

These links are routinely monitored and updated to provide the most current information available.

GLOSSARY

draft
A system by which sports leagues divide up new talent.

rookie
A first-year player.

shifty
Able to quickly move back and forth to avoid defenders.

snap
When the center passes the ball to the quarterback to start a play.

Swiss Army knife
A pocketknife that combines multiple tools, such as a knife, screwdriver, and scissors.

unique
One of a kind.

yards from scrimmage
Combined rushing and receiving yards.

INDEX